LUCIE ATTWELL'S
Little one's Book
of
PRAYERS

Presented
to

Scott Dowling

From

Good News Club.

Christian Literature Crusade
51, The Dean, Alresford, Hants.

First published 1975
Reprinted 1982, 1983, 1984, 1985

Published by Deans International Publishing
52-54 Southwark Street, London SE1 1UA
A division of The Hamlyn Publishing Group Limited
London · New York · Sydney · Toronto

Illustrations Copyright © Mabel Lucie Attwell 1975

ISBN 0 603 01602 2

Printed and bound in Great Britain by
Purnell and Sons (Book Production) Ltd., Paulton, Bristol.
Member of BPCC plc

LITTLE Lamb, who made thee?
    Dost thou know who made thee?
Gave thee life and bid thee feed,
By the stream and o'er the mead—
Gave thee clothing of delight,
Softest clothing, woolly bright,
Gave thee such a tender voice,
Making all the vales rejoice—

Little Lamb, who made thee?
Dost thou know who made thee?

PRAISE God from whom all blessings flow,
Praise Him, all creatures here below,
Praise Him above, the heavenly host,
Praise Father, Son and Holy Ghost.

I LOVE to hear the story
  Which angel voices tell,
How once the King of glory
  Came down on earth to dwell.
I am both weak and human
  But this I surely know,
The Lord came down to save me,
  Because he loved me so.

I'm glad my blessed Saviour
  Was once a child like me,
To show how pure and holy
  His little ones might be;
And if I try to follow
  His footsteps here below,
He never will forsake me,
  Because he loves me so.

HERE a little child I stand
Heaving up my either hand.
Cold as paddocks though they be,
Here I lift them up to thee
For a benison to fall
On our meat and on us all.

STILL the night, holy the night,
  Sleeps the world, hid from sight.
Mary and Joseph in stable bare
Watch o'er the Child beloved and fair,
Sleeping in heavenly rest.

Still the night, holy the night.
Shepherds first saw the light,
Heard resounding clear and long,
Far and near, the angel-song.
Christ the Redeemer is here.

Still the night, holy the night.
Son of God, O how bright
Love is smiling from thy face.
Strikes for us now the hour of grace,
Saviour, since thou art born!

I SAW a robin on a spade
    And he was something
        You had made.
A furry rabbit 'neath a tree,
An elephant, a bumble-bee.
Dear Lord, I know you made
        them all,
The biggest and the very
        small.

HUSH, my dear, lie still and slumber.
   Holy angels guard thy bed.
Heavenly blessings without number
Gently falling on thy head.

O COME let us sing unto the Lord;
   Let us make a joyful noise
      to the rock of our salvation.

Let us come before his presence
   with thanksgiving and make a joyful noise
      unto him with psalms.

For the Lord is a great God, and a
   great King above all gods.

In his hand are the deep places of the earth;
The strength of the hills is his also.

The sea is his, and he made it;
And his hands formed the dry land.

      O come, let us wor-
         ship and bow
            down;
      Let us kneel before
         the Lord our
            maker.

LORD, make us glad for every day.
   For all the fun that comes our way.
For work and games and trees and flowers
   and wind and sunshine,
Dew and showers.

For houses and the busy street,
For family and friends we meet.
For everything we see and do
Is good—because it comes from you.

OUR Father which art in Heaven
   Hallowed be Thy name.
Thy kingdom come.
Thy will be done, in earth as it is
   in Heaven.
Give us this day our daily bread
And forgive us our trespasses,
As we forgive them that trespass
   against us.
And lead us not into temptation;
But deliver us from evil.
For Thine is the Kingdom,
The power and the glory
For ever and ever.
                    Amen.

HELP me do the things I should,
To be to others kind and good.
In all my work, and all my play—
To grow more loving every day.

O HOLY Jesus, most merciful Redeemer,
Friend and Brother,
May I see Thee more clearly,
Love Thee more dearly,
And follow Thee more nearly,
Day by day.

ALL praise and thanks to God
    The Father now be given,
The Son, and him who reigns
With them in highest heaven.
The one eternal God,
Whom earth and heaven adore,
For thus it was, is now,
And shall be evermore.

LORD, keep us safe this night,
    Secure from all our fears.
May angels guard us while we sleep
Till morning light appears.

JESUS, I offer Thee this day
All my thoughts and work and
play.
Let me be good as good can be,
Gentle, loving, kind like Thee.

FOR what we are about to receive
May the Lord make us truly
thankful,
And keep us ever mindful of the
needs of others.

MAKE a joyful noise to the Lord, all
    ye lands!
Serve the Lord with gladness:
Come before his presence with singing.
Know ye that the Lord is God:
It is he that hath made us, and not we
    ourselves;
We are his people, and the sheep of his pasture.
Enter into his gates with thanksgiving, and
    into his courts with praise:
Be thankful unto him, and bless his name.
For the Lord is good; his mercy everlasting;
And his truth endureth to all generations.

THE Grace of our Lord Jesus Christ
And the love of God
And the fellowship of the Holy Spirit,
Be with us now and evermore. Amen.